WWW.2BEKNOWN.COM

2BEKNOWN
CONSULTING CONTACTS CONNECTIONS

„May "Direct Recruiting" not only qualify your business but qualify your life!"
Alexander Riedl

www.2beknown.com

This book covers the complete methodology of 2BEKNOWN. It is unique and aims to provide the standard guideline and workbook for the active recruiter or people canvassing for customers.

Contributors:

- **Rainer von Massenbach** and **Tobias Schlosser** are the founders of this effective method. Extensive experience about direct recruiting and personal topics have found their way into this book through them.

- **Alexander Riedl** has collected and edited this experience and made this book available.

- Almost 80.000 people who were approached and whose responses helped to develop this methodology.

- Many participants in our workshops and seminars who helped to formulate a capacious method: **The 2BEKNOWN method.**

CONTENTS

THE 2BEKNOWN-METHOD

PREFACE

You will fail completely if you are not capable of contacting people anytime, anywhere!

Did I catch your attention?

I thought so, because making contact is a marginal topic within any business. You would not read this book if you didn't agree.

If you want to get in shape you need a fitness plan. If you want to build a house you need blueprints.
So what do you think is required to build up contacts?
The 2BEKNOWN method is a tried and tested method. It is designed specifically to develop these skills.

It is no secret that Rainer von Massenbach and Tobias Schlosser are distinguished experts in the field of direct recruiting. Therefore many colleges and partners have asked them about their methods. They began to give courses and workshops privately and noticed the great impact on their participant's' success.

This book is not written to be read and then put away. Consider it as a workbook and companion on your journey to become a successful recruiter and contact man. Mark important notes! Try out everything even if it seems a little weird at the beginning. If you work on your skills on a daily basis you will notice how new potentials emerge and a new understanding of the method develops.

FOUNDERS OF THE 2BEKNOWN METHOD

Rainer Gemmingen Freiherr von Massenbach

Born into a noble family, a classical and straight career, supported by my family's status seemed to be the right thing for me. But an apprenticeship in a bank, university and then becoming a lawyer or management consultant did not feature among my options.

Just shortly after completing my Abitur (USA: High School + two years of college GB: A-Levels) my conservative family was shocked by my "MLM-Adventures".

In an unusual, though very direct manner, I was recruited by my friend and mentor Tobias Schlosser, who filled me with enthusiasm and with the idea of a career as financial advisor.

Highly motivated by the opportunities on offer and by my will to become a successful entrepreneur, I achieved immense successes within my financial services company.

Through my unconventional way of contacting people anytime and anywhere and to multiply this capacity, I was able to establish persistent growth of my sales team.

I developed the idea to formulate my experience and knowledge of this time in a form that enables every entrepreneur and independent Multi Level Marketing agent to use and profit from it. One method that is unique but universal: the 2BEKNOWN method.

In this field my extraordinary approaches and unconventional solutions give me the passion to communicate.

I wish you this passion with all your assignments and tasks of your life.

Sincerely,

Rainer von Massenbach

2BEKNOWN
CONSULTING CONTACTS CONNECTIONS

„Anybody who can contact people anytime and anywhere has to be worried about his financial situation ever again!"

Rainer von Massenbach – 2BEKNOWN

Tobias Schlosser

Raised in Leipzig, I garnered experience in motivating and communicating as a physiotherapist, primarily and within the health and fitness sector.

Whilst studying, I established contacts with the competitive economy and decided on a career as a multi level marketer. Having overcome the initial difficulties associated with conventional methods, I managed to realign the business into a positive direction.
Recruiting my first partners ignited my passion for group development by means of professional and classy ways of addressing people as well as the art of direct recruiting.

I cultivated this art in countless conversations and this enabled me the possibility to build huge groups in Leipzig and Munich.

To maintain this success, I had to find a way of transferring my experience and knowledge to my employees and co-workers. I Soon became widely known as a specialist for communication and recruitment skills and had to give lectures with large numbers of attendees.

More than five years ago I brought Rainer von Massenbach, my friend and business partner into my branch, using direct recruiting.

The skill and passion to contact people anywhere and anytime is therefore the basis of today's seminar and workshop concept of 2BEKNOWN.

Dare to try it!

Sincerely,

Tobias Schlosser

„If you cannot talk about your business and convince people about it, distribution is the wrong thing for you."
Tobias Schlosser – 2BEKNOWN

DIRECT ACQUISITION

Editorial note:
The German word "Fremdkontakt" covers more than "Direct Recruiting".
It refers to a general way of talking to strangers without any connection
to the stranger or the business.
It covers recruiting and selling situations and even privately motivated
contacting.
Though "Direct Recruiting" is mainly used in this translated book, "Direct
Acquisition" transfers a more precise translation.

We intensively studied many methods of MLM and distributing types and
their ways to gain contacts. To exclude the pure skill of making contacts
we found the following definition as fitting:

*"Direct Acquisition enables you to get in contact with people at
anytime, anywhere. It is a learnable social skill geared aims to
exchanging contact data when both parties have interest after
introducing a business/product in the shortest time possible.
Performed correctly it should be applicable in any situation with
fun and sophistication."*

Learning the ability of Direct Acquisition will change all aspects of your
life for the better. By observing the reactions during your first attempts
you will find patterns which will lead you to enhance your success rate
and to try out new varieties. Practise will give you not only new business
contacts but also private ones. Not every contact will be suitable for your
business, but some contacts are so interesting that friendships or even
more develop from direct contacting.
No matter what kind of business you are in – the ability to arouse interest
will bring you successful!

Let 2BEKNOWN be your assistant and mentor to guide you to a successful
life.

"The ability to contact people directly is worth millions!"
CEO of a company to whom we are consultants

THE BORN DIRECT RECRUITER

Direct contacting is actually a natural reaction.
Imagine sitting in a café and watching the perfect candidate for your business on the next table enjoying coffee.
After a while the two of you talk about life in general and as you are talking about your business you evoke interest.
You are exchanging numbers and leave the café.

Did you notice? That was a direct contact!

But how often does this happen? Once a week? Once a month?
That is what we deal with at 2BEKNOWN. Our method enables you to have ten of those contacts - every day.

It is important to know that neither Rainer von Massenbach nor Tobias Schlosser was born with this skill. Another fact is: Most people who state they have such skills actually do. Ego and pride are often involved.

Everyone can talk to someone once in a while. If the situation is right you might get a telephone number coincidently. But a large number of MLM participants don't even know what a classy direct contact looks like.
No one likes to admit that the most natural contact – human to human – is a problem for almost everyone.

THE 2BEKNOWN-METHOD

PART 1
THE ORIGIN OF THE 2BEKNOWN-METHOD

There are people who are able to communicate in different situations with others. They are always the centre of attention, always have interesting stories to tell. These people will always be successful. They are interesting and good storytellers – it seems that their life is always more interesting than all the James Bond movies put together.
Rainer von Massenbach was not like that. He was the typical loser in the corner of every party and it looked like sorting matches would be his hobby.

Someone like Rainer von Massenbach was the "Anti-Socializer". The dress-code "Idiot" had his picture as a reference. To talk to strangers – to recruit strangers was such a remote possibility; it wasn't even worth a try.

At this point nobody imagined he would become the man he is today.
One day Tobias Schlosser gave him a highly motivated talk, even though he had just lost all of his employees in Leipzig.
With nothing more than 100 Euros in cash, 2 suits, 3 pairs of underwear, 4 shirts and a black Mercedes he managed to reach his aim.

Had he listened to the warnings of his family and friends, he would have never dared to walk this path and move to Munich.
But in his very first week he met Rainer von Massenbach. A highly motivated "contacting machine" with a hairy chest met a student with no social skills and the extravagance of a snail.

But numbers were exchanged and they arranged a meeting.

The rest, as they say, is history.

Tobias Schlosser remembers the very first day in Munich:

"It was a sunny day in June and I sat behind the steering weal of my Mercedes on the 'Autobahn' to Munich. New city - new fortune.
My cell phone kept ringing, family and friends reminding me constantly of the stupidity on which I am about to embark. As if I had decided to sell refrigerators to Eskimos. I was always the same: "Being from Eastern Germany you won't understand a single word in Munich."
And of course the Eastern German dialect and Bavarian are indeed the most different German dialects within the German speaking world. "The market in Munich is overcrowded." "You don't know anybody there." "They are different and follo other rules." …

I ignored all this advice and hit the gas leavinge every negative thought behind. You need a lot of gas at 220 kilometres an hour (approx. 137 mph). I had to stop for some gas and noticed a polished Audi A8 next to a well-dressed man who was refuelling this beauty.

I: "Hi. Are you from Munich?" (The licence plate said M for Munich)
He: "Yes, I am", he answered with a friendly smile.

Let's give it a try, I thought:
I: "I've just arrived in Munich and intend to expand my business here. You look like a successful man. May I ask what your profession is?"
He: "I am a self-employed architect."
I: "Self-employed? Good! Personally I prefer to work with self-employed entrepreneurs. So I wonder: Are you generally open to new business ideas?"
He: "Yes, but what exactly are you talking about?"

I handed him my business card.
He: "Oh, that insurance company."
I: "Yes, I am about to develop a new branch office and am looking for people with leadership qualities. I am responsible for marketing organisation, personnel development and wholesale. Are you open to a good offer?"
He: (laughs) "I still don't know what you mean, but let's have a talk together."
I: "That's why I'm giving you my business card. Let's talk. Do you have your business card along?"
He: "Of course."

He handed me his card and I went on:
>*"Good. I'm going to be in Stuttgart for a few days, but I will call you when I am back in Munich."*

He: "Sounds good."
I: "See you soon then. Good bye."

I left and thought: This is the start of a new 'cell' in Munich. I drove on and got into Munich shortly after. I stopped next to the first person that suited my expectations and pulled down the window:
>*"Hi, can you help me for a minute..."*

Before I finally met my colleague I had 25 new contacts. The market is full? Not if you ask me!
"Now, how was your journey?", was the first thing I was asked.
"I collected 25 numbers!"
The office was quiet and everyone stared at me as if I were the incredible Hulk, holding a Boeing 747 in my bare hands. Within the next two days I collected another 50 numbers and started to recruit those candidates four days after I arrived. I had about 8-10 appointments a day and managed to develop a respective team in a very short period. THROUGH DIRECT RECRUITING."

Rainer von Massenbach and Tobias Schlosser worked together for two years within a financial MLM and developed a team of 120 active members and several offices. This was only possible through direct recruiting.

Tobias Schlosser learned the basics of direct recruiting back in Leipzig, former Eastern Germany, and improved and developed this art together with Rainer von Massenbach. Old rules were tried out and redefined during thousands of direct addresses.

Some patterns broke and had to be reconsidered, others seemed to work everywhere. As the success became clearly visible, colleagues asked for advice and "tricks". They held small workshops and presentations until they agreed: "Training direct recruiting is going to be our main business. Our method is learnable, it works everywhere and everyone can draw immediate benefit from advantage out of it. Everyone can find business partners with fun and ease!"

The 2BEKNOWN method is a dynamic process.

When you learn the art of direct recruiting you will take the same steps as everyone else, but you will develop your own unique style.Every workshop demonstrates how certain "tricks" develop into personal models. While observing Tobias Schlosser, for example, you will notice that he harrumphs before starting a conversation, while Rainer von Massenbach raises his hand like a schoolboy.

YOUR ULTIMATE TASK WITHIN MARKETING

TO GENERATE GROWTH AND SALES VOLUME

YOUR MAIN DISCIPLINES:

SELLING   RECRUITING PERSONNEL

Selling: Each market centres on selling. Without selling there is no product. Without selling there is no money.

Recruiting Personnel: The success of your method will dictate whether your team grows or shrinks. Those who do not use a specific system are destined for coincidence.

Don't forget: Every market is a dynamic business and rejuvenates itself through constant re-organization.

Quick yet sustained growth is only possible only through constant recruiting. The used system should be a repeatable method.

There is a new trend within multi-level-marketing that prefers broad structures which provide security and more money. Therefore even old hands should reconsider the importance of direct recruiting and open up towards new methods.

There are many sellers who are able to reach almost 90% of their costumers, and great leaders who motivate their disciples every day. But the strongest leader needs personnel, the best seller needs customers: it is essential to make contacts.

Without contacts, without personnel or customers, it's over. Your business is dead.

LOOKING INTO THE FUTURE OF YOUR BUSINESS

A student knows a student knows a student... Do you know what I mean?

Assuming that every person tends to know people of the same social status, we are facing the problem that contact without any interest for you will lead to another contact of the same value. Even worse - most recommendations are declining. If any given contact knows people who'se social status can be divided into A (highest social status), B and C (lowest social status) it is likely that he gives us contacts out of class B or C, but rarely out of class A.

This is a form of unconscious self-protection. If the person asked is lacking in belief, the A-contact will stay untouched. But our aim at is to enhance social status when recruiting. That is why direct recruiting offers the potential to break this chain of „downward recruiting": you can choose the person you want to win for your business.

Rainer von Massenbach talks about his personal background:

"I was never the perfect member of an MLM business. I wasn't what can be considered as popular in school. I wasn't even the centre of my own birthday parties. My social circle was very small.
My only contacts were some classmates, and that was my whole potential.

I started to have appointments with them, but students are not really the perfect target group for a MLM in the financial sector. After a couple of discussions, all I had collected were virtually useless recommendations and numbers.
But to gather some numbers by recommendation was the only way to increase potential. What I also hated was having to beg for those recommendations. I didn't offer, I begged for names and numbers.
Even worse were my attempts to simply call strangers to make some appointments. Those who actually came were broke and could not even afford our first seminar.

To be frank: Those people were even of a lower status than I was.
I noticed that direct recruiting worked for some colleagues, but I wasn't brave enough to speak to a total stranger about my business. Tobias Schlosser took me by the hand: I learned my first steps with him. His stringent methods worked for me, but are they repeatable for everyone?

My career as a recruiter started like this:
I stood in a bank with Tobias Schlosser while an attractive businesswoman was using the ATM. Back then, approaching her directly would have been the last thing on my mind.

Tobias walked towards her and said: "Hello, my colleague wants to ask you something."
Then he turned around and saw my heart in my boots. I was frozen. My lungs screamed for some air as I stopped breathing for a while. I can't remember what I said, but I said something.
As we left the bank, Tobias repeated his merciless game. Again and again.

That is how I learned direct recruiting. But is this method repeatable, multipliable? We had to find a method that is easy and repeatable for everyone."

Our society develops a so called "cocooning" trend. The insecure public is avoided and social contacts are reduced or substituted by virtual contacts. Only few but intense social contacts are kept.

It appears that we increasingly decide who can get into contact with us and who can't. You are a victim of "cocooning" as soon as you feel strange if your display shows 'withheld' when the phone rings.

Rainer von Massenbach on Advertisement and "Cocooning"

"Direct recruiting is brilliant because I reach out to people in a new way. Every day I find 20 spam mails in my inbox – in the morning alone. In my car, I hear commercials on the radio and see hundreds of advertisements before I even arrive at work. There are even advertisements on my pen, my cup and almost everything I use at work.

This kind of advertisement only works en masse. It takes years and millions to influence the consumer through "public relations". And people are getting used to that: their barriers to communication are becoming harder to break down. This filter is irrelevant when it comes to direct recruiting!

Social networking pages in the internet can be configured to the extent to which I am contactable. If I don't see a number, I don't answer the phone. Having had call-centre agents myself, I expect the call agent to identify himself."

None of these problems apply to direct recruiting. You can recruit without recommendations on a high social level, without costs or detour.

"This gave me the idea of combining the "contacting power" of Tobias Schlosser and the deficits of a shy person such as myself and form a guide that provides everyone with the necessary tools for direct recruiting."

HIGH POTENTIALS

High potentials are people who are business wise, personally, socially or financially above average. It is an important experience to address people of a high social status.

As Rainer von Massenbach explains:

"Our experience tells us that this group reacts surprisingly positively to direct recruiting, if it is performed on a high level.
Surprising these people often generates an incredible outspokenness. And you can talk to them frankly without the intervention of secretaries."

Of course it is also very interesting to talk to people you would normally never meet. Rainer von Massenbach and Tobias Schlosser are taking every opportunity to chat about personality and business with "high potentials", resulting in a huge number of business cards in their "wealthy contacts" -folder.
Almost all were direct contacts.

The correct level is very important when you are addressing high potentials. Acting as a stuck- up opportunity provider will not work, but as an equal and respectful potential ssible partner will.
Don't be arrogant, even if your opposite is overweening. Just go away without wasting your time on discussion.

Recruit your target group and concentrate on things that take your business forward. Be aware that people who seem to have no need are sometimes very open to new ideas.
If not it is always training and experience.

Tobias Schlosser about contacting higher potentials:

Management consultants or managers in leading positions tend to earn more than the average worker. Their reputation is higher, they have more responsibility and their companies give them benefits.

But responsibility often comes with pressure. Personal freedom and time are cut until they have their company's property.
Sometimes that is why even high potentials are unsatisfied and search for improvement.
Let's face it: improvement does not necessarily mean more money!

Getting back to the issue at hand:
In the beginning I started to address the "neckties" and "office ladies" only to destroy my fears. But then I noticed that high potentials are more open than most others. Some colleagues and I started a competition: who will get more and better top-managers.
We simply named a minimum (e.g. cars, neckties, brief case) that possible contacts had to have. One thing was always the same: the fancier, the better!

We walked on one of the worlds most expensive shopping streets, for instance, and talked to people who wore dresses that were more expensive than our cars, and who used cell phones that could have financed our yearly vacation.

These campaigns had extraordinary results and many business contacts were generated.
I have to admit at this point, that 90% of them did not work with us in the end, but many of them became customers. Given what I know now I think I would have had more of them working for me.

The important thing is that we had the time to talk to them about our business during an appointment. We managed to meet them in our office by applying what is today called the 2BEKNOWN method.

As an example I would like to tell you what kind of people we talked to back then.

We had:

- Meetings with employees of Germany's biggest banks (from regular counter staff to branch managers)

- Successfully recruited fund managers

- Meetings with successful entrepreneurs who served on boards of directors

- Meetings with famous actors and sports personalities

- Job interviews with lawyers, engineers...

- Cooperation with controllers, tax consultants...

- Meetings with management consultants

Much later, after I analyzed these meetings, I realized that they all had two things in common:

1. They all searched for improvement! (this has nothing to do with social status, 80% are always searching!)

2. The way we addressed them met their standards of quality. (We often heard: "You are not the first one talking to me about this, but never in that way.")

*"**This skill should be cultivated.**"*
Reaction of a director of a DAX-company

PART 2
THE RECRUITER`S PERSONALITY

If someone hands over his telephone number it should not be because he feels pity for you. But why does someone hear what you have to say? Buys your products? Is interested in your words?

You offer a benefit! You are able to provide advantages of which the person was unaware.
No matter if you can offer a job on the side or financial freedom, if you have something for just a few hours or a full time job. Why do YOU work within your team, your company today?
You like to schedule your own time? You want to become a millionaire?

Whatever it is, that is what you have to communicate. The following pages look at your opportunities. Opportunities that allow you to be a communicative person, a magnetic personality.

Don't be afraid of defeat and denial. Find out what you are looking for. Bring a benefit into the life of everyone you are talking to. And win that person for you and your business.
Sympathy is a key qualification for your business – for ANY business. If we like someone we talk about everything. Let people like you.

„If there is any one secret of success, it lies in the ability to get the other person's point of view and see things from that person's angle as well as from your own. "
Henry Ford

THE RECRUITER'S ATTITUDE

In the early days I met colleagues who went about direct recruiting like this:

They drove Porsches, pulled up next to young men and asked them if they want to earn some money.
That was enough to get their numbers.
But not every reader might have a 150000 € car and is interested in 20-year-olds that are motivated by that.
Long-lasting business relations -- these are what we want.

But the „Porsche-Approach" contains important components of direct recruiting: one's own status has to be fitting!

You are offering, not begging, not wanting and not need to convince a certain individual.
You are a great person with a good business opportunity to offer.
(If you don't agree here, you will fail - regardless of your skills and methods.)

Whether the person you are talking to takes up your offer or not is his or her decision.
Don't sell yourself below value. They say: „A won discussion is a lost sell".
This is applicable for recruiting as well.
Be friendly but efficient. If someone has only negative answers for you, don't discuss - move on. You don't need negative people for your business.

REJECTION AND THE FEAR OF TALKING TO STRANGERS

Being rejected will not harm you. If you think about it, nothing can happen. But why does rejection hurt us, even when that rejection comes from total strangers? To understand this, we have to go back to the roots of our social behaviour.

Living in a Stone Age community meant living in a very small circle. If someone tried to get in contact with someone, rejection was a threat. Everyone within the group would know about it and the social status might have suffered. This decrease meant a lower chance of mating. So the fear of being rejected is based on the instinct to spread our genes. The instinct of self preservation.

Of course this is ridiculous nowadays, but our brains are still programmed in this manner.
Today's communities are big and we are free to leave certain groups and join a different ones. Our status is marked by different means and being rejected feeds only a rudimentary fear.

But how can we avoid being rejected?

The answer is simple: You can't. You can just learn to cope with it. It can't be a solution to „cocoon" yourself. Not for you, personally, and definitely not for your business. What you can do is to accept your vulnerability. If you are rejected, analyze why and learn from it.
Be honest with yourself: Have you been rejected often? Or is the imagination of being rejected worse?
Every day you will be rejected in this business. But you will learn how to cope with it, and you will get better and better.

IDENTIFICATION

Rainer von Massenbach talks about his own experience:

„There was one vendor in our company I avoided. Not because I didn't like him, or because he was unfriendly, he sold me a savings plan whenever I talked to him.
I called them insurance policies, but he spoke about ways of fulfilling dreams. He slobbered about the freedom security brings.
The difference between him and others was simple: IDENTIFICATION!

To be successful and to be able to achieve your goals you have to identify with what you are doing. 100%. If it is less, then you may as well lock yourself up in the basement with a bottle of wine and think about what you are doing.
What benefits does your product, your business reap? What are you offering to the people, to your customers?
If you can identify with your business, it will be felt immediately. Your surroundings will respond. It is easy to motivate those you want to motivate. Be serious about your work, and success will follow suit.

If I think about the Soccer World Championship in 2006, I remember how all of Germany questioned the methods of our national trainer. But he stuck to his methods and did not let himself get irritated.
Most of us would have listened to the others - would have questioned ourselves.
But if you are really doing what you want to do, you will allure people around you and will have the aura of success.

Many of those I recruited successfully had been contacted by the same company before without any results. They reason why they were open to my approach because I identified with what I was doing.
I was able to stand up for my company - every time and everywhere."

GOALS TO BOOST YOUR EGO

Define your goals. You must have heard this a thousand times, but it eventually sinks in time.

Rainer von Massenbach about his favourite topic:

„Do you have a clear aim? In thousands of workshops and meetings I asked this question and only half of the attendees raised their hands. I asked those people to define their goals clearly and after about four questions most of them couldn't answer precisely anymore. They didn't know if their own house should have 4 or 5 rooms, or if their car is supposed to be black or white.

Why? I think a defined goal is essential. Why do you get out of bed, if you don't know why? Everyone has goals, but not everyone is aware of them. There is no sense in your life, if you don't have goals.

Think of successful people. Do you think Bill Gates didn`t know where he wanted to go when he started working on his first projects? Every successful man and women is determined. They know what they want and what they work for. If you talk to them, you will notice immediately that they have plans.
When I asked high potentials why they agreed to meet me, they said because they think I know what I want.
If you know what you want, people will listen to you, they will work with or for you.

Kids are like that. They are motivated and strenuous until they get what they want. We learned to postpone or abandon our wishes for no reason. We can't cry anymore to fulfil our will, but we must learn to have that passion again. Why have we been taught to level our needs with the mass?

We lost our purposefulness and we have to get it back to be successful. Be honest: you want more than the average life. Everyone wants more, but no one dares to say it.

Every time something didn't work out, every time I was rejected while direct recruiting, I gained new energy from my goals. Plan your goal! Plan activities for each day you are working on them.
Important: Plan activities, not results!"

Tobias Schlosser on Identification and goals

„I drive along Leipzig in Sportswear in my Trabi, with it's charm of communist poverty. I just want to see what happened during the last 5 months since I left home. I have to stop at a traffic light and there' is this man with a radiating drive, waiting for the light to turn green. I immediately noticed that I had to talk to him, but my ego kept telling me:

- *Your car is ridiculous!*

- *You are not dressed well at all!*

- *You have just been to the fitness studio and are probably smelly!*

- *You are not working at the moment!*

- *A traffic light is not a good spot to start a chat!*

- *Leipzig! You are working in Munich, why do you want to meet someone from Leipzig?*

I don't know why but I still started to pull down the window with the dangerously dickey crank handle:

> *„Hello", I screamed.*

He looked at me and probably expected to be asked for directions.
But I had other things in mind:

I: *„Maybe you can help me. But I don't need directions."*

He: *„How can I help you?"*

I: *„I might not look like it now, but I am actually developing a branch office of my company here. Are you from around here?"*

He: *„Yes"*

I: *„What is your profession?"*

He: *„I am studying sport science."*

I: *„Perfect. I am looking for some students that could help me out when it comes to team supervision and marketing. Are you up for earning good money on the side?"*

He: *„Yes, what branch?"*

I: *„I work for an insurance company and am responsible for development and personnel."*

He: *„What exactly are you doing? I still don't get it."*

I: „That's ok. Let us talk some other time, and then I can explain everything to you. The traffic light is not the right atmosphere to talk about money and career."

He: „OK"

I: „Here, use my pen to write down your number."

He: „Sure:"

He wrote down his number...

This tale proves that success has nothing to do with the correct surrounding, wear or status.

With bravery, motivation and the right kind of approach everything can be achieved.

It proves that there are many reasons not to start an attempt of direct recruiting in your mind, but one reason that is essential:

Visualization of your aim and the heart to go for it!

SCHEDULE ACTIVITIES – NOT RESULTS

We all know those days when everything just turns out automatically. But there are days when nothing works at all. You have to accept that in order to avoid frustration. That is why it is helpful to plan activities instead of results. You are responsible for activities, results may vary. Results may also be luck.

Let's say you planned to collect 10 numbers, but the weather is bad. It rains cats and dogs. It will be quite difficult now to fulfil your goal. It would have been better to formulate your plan for the day like this: contact 10 people regardless of their reaction.
This is possible every day. Even on rainy days you will have 2-3 numbers afterwards.

This is the difference:

Goal 1: Collect 10 Numbers in 4 hours
Result: 6 numbers

Goal 2: Talk to 10 candidates about your business in 4 hours
Result: 3 numbers

You might think that the first result is better, but you did not achieve your goal. The second goal may only have resulted in 3 numbers, but you achieved your goal for the day. There is no frustration. You will stay motivated and be happier. After all, you can't be successful if you are not having fun!

Schedule activities, not results!

BODY LANGUAGE AND VOICE

This is an important point. More important then what you say is how you say it. If someone whispers and looks at his shoes he will not be worth listening to. How would you like to be talked to? Think about it – and then speak like that! Self-assured and openly.

Look into the face of everyone you are talking to. Stand or walk straight and use a clear voice. And one more thing: smile!

ABOUT SMILING

Smiling is a present you should give away more often. It does not cost you anything, but always generates positive feedback. It's also good for you, you will feel better.
Just walk through your neighbourhood and look for people who are smiling. Most of your neighbours will stare emotionless or even stressed.

Are you a zombie like that? Someone who is a witness to eternal pain?

Smile! Friendly people are not rejected.

Start searching for people with a happy appearance. Then look at them and smile. If they are smiling back, say "hello". You will be surprised by the reactions.

A winning smile is worth more than 100,.000 well-chosen words.
Did this ever happen to you?, You're walking through the city and somebody is courteous to you.

When the person passed you, your eyes met and there it was – this special moment:
This magic between total strangers. That feeling of knowing someone.
You thought you should get to know this person. On most occasions you will let this moment pass and you will go on with your every day life.
This book will also give you the opportunity to act in those situations.

„There is no security in life – just opportunity."
Tobias Schlosser

ANALOGY TESTS

Whoever you are talking to is going to be confronted with a new situation. You are a stranger who just started a conversation about life-changing opportunities. That is not "normal".

This raises some questions - sometimes uncomfortable and weird questions. Many of our workshop's attendees noticed that those questions are often asked by highly qualified candidates. For a newbie, sceptical questions about the product, company or the system can be quite a task. Experienced recruiters know that these candidates have the highest quality.

People who give away their numbers without hesitation don't think about what they are doing. Or they are too surprised.

Would you give away your number after 20 seconds with a total stranger? Maybe. Maybe not. But I would ask some questions before I give away my name and number.

So be aware: good candidates will ask questions! They have experience, they are doing business, they are working and they learned not to give away their number to just anybody. Good candidates can decide with whom they want to get in contact with. If someone offers them a business opportunity without being self-assured, without a well-formulated benefit for them, they won't give away their numbers.

We call these questions analogy tests as they aim at finding out who you are and what you stand for. These questions will reveal whether you are standing up for your business and whether the intention in your offer is solid. And here is the tricky problem. If you are answering too many questions, you won't be interesting anymore. But if you are apparently hiding information you will disqualify yourself.

So think about the information you want to give away ahead of time – and stick to that concept. Sometimes it is wiser to "lose" a direct recruiting attempt than being left without a number after being drawn out.

Let yourself and your business be tested. And show your qualities. Be friendly and give your best, but don't lose your concept.

One more thing: Don't mix up contacts that are just collecting information with those who are interested. Don't waste your time.

UNCOMFORTABLE SITUATIONS AND CONFRONTATIONS

Every social interaction exposes you the risk of uncomfortable situations. And direct recruiting is no exception.
You could speak to a man who has just been left by his wife, lost a fortune on the stock market and missed his train to work. No matter how good you are, in some situations your opponent might be unfriendly and stressed!

Sometimes it's just about timing. You cannot know what happened, so you have to take those risks. Never forget that it might have nothing to do with anything you can influence. In those cases, it has nothing to do with you or your business; it is just the wrong time.

But that very person could have become a good team member if the situation was different, so:

- Have an open and positive attitude

- Avoid confrontations and concentrate on your goal

- Don't let yourself be pulled into senseless discussions

- Don't be sad as if it were a big deal – it's not

- If someone is not interested, say goodbye and leave; stay friendly

If you should meet again, be friendly and greet. This could be the start of a conversation with a surprisingly positive outcome!

PART 3

IMPORTANT FACTS ON DIRECT RECRUITING

YOU WILL HAVE TO INVEST!

In order to become a successful recruiter you have to realize that direct contacting is a social skill - a learnable social skill. You will have to invest in that learning process, regardless of the skills you have achieved so far.

Investments:

- **Time:** To learn a new skill, time is essential. The module system (Part 5) will give you the tools to progress in your day to day training.

- **Money:** The 2BEKNOWN method requires only a pen and a piece of paper. So you'd better invest your money in your appearance, which will bring better results than other utensils.

- **Emotional Investment:** Realize that you are LEARNING a new skill. If you feel the learning process, you will be able to accept setbacks.

APPEARANCE

I want you to look like a model! I want you to wear a tailored suit, fitness training at least 4 times a week and buy cosmetics once a week.

Only kidding. I just want you to take care of your body - take care of your appearance. It may not need mentioning, but I have to say that I have experienced more or less marginal deficits in this regard. The first thing that is noticed, when two people meet is each other's appearance.
It doesn't matter whether you are very attractive or whether you are wearing an expensive suit or dress, what does matter is a clean and proper appearance. A nice pullover with jeans is still better than a worn-out suit with a yellowed tie.

Do me one favour: Go to a hairdresser once in a while and (as a man) shave that wool of your face. No one wants to talk to someone about business opportunities if that person looks like he doesn't even own a mirror.

And last but not least, you will feel better. It will be easier to talk to candidates if you are feeling clean.

ALONE, IN PAIRS OR AS A GROUP?

Many have asked me, if it is better to recruit alone or in a group. Everyone has his own favourite situation. In every day life, you are likely to be on your own.

However, to learn the art of direct recruiting, I suggest you getting someone to practice with a sparring partner. It can be a lot of fun to experience success and work on defeats together. That' is why we are forming groups in our workshops to hunt for numbers.

So find someone in your team, organize a group or do it on your own. Direct contacting is meant to be fun, broaden your horizon and, of course, give you enough contacts to succeed in your business.

CONTACTING ACTIVITY RULES

If you decided to learn in a group, agree on some rules. It is strange for others if you jump on them in a wild pack of five recruiters. Whoever finds an interesting person should look for an identifying feature and, for example, say: „The guy in the yellow jacket is mine!" The others will know that you are going to start the conversation.

Another important rule: two recruiters are the maximum to start a conversation. If you are contacting in a group, never let more than one group member join a conversation. If a bigger group just stands there in front of a stranger, looking at him like a new attraction in Disney World, the contact might feel uneasy. But even if two recruiters are in one conversation, only one of them should speak.

A rule for good friendship: Whoever starts to contact someone gets his or her number! You may agree on some exceptions. In a learning process a „trainer" might get involved and collect the number, to hand it to a newbie afterwards. In our workshops we often arrange groups of three, consisting of one instructor and two attendees.

HOI POLLOI OR FISHING FOR PRINCES

Direct contracting and selling have one thing in common: There can never be a 100% success-rate.
Logically, this can never happen!

Even very successful recruiters like Tobias Schlosser can never get every person's number. But talking about rates, there are two main options when it comes to the 2BEKNOWN method. Your business or product will dictate which one makes more sense for you.

The hoi polloi selection:
You can talk to as many people as possible with just few criteria that have to be fulfilled. Let's say, you are contacting every person between 20 and 50 years of age wherever you are. This will lead to a great number of potential candidates.

The fishing for princes selection:
You have a strongly defined target group and will therefore find fitting candidates from a smaller group.
Let's say you are contacting men in suits between 35 and 45 years of age on an expensive shopping street if they greet back when you say hello. These criteria mean you will speak less people but most of them might suit your needs.

It is your decision how you define your selection. Try out both methods and then improve the one that reflects you and your business best.

In most MLM systems you will have to become a trainer for others at some point. That is why you should practice both selection methods to provide what is needed in your team.

HOW DO I DEFINE MY TARGET GROUP?

To whom you talk to is depends on how you feel comfortable. A bad attempt performed in a friendly way is always more likely to be successful than an arrogant yet rhetorically perfect conversation.
In order to find out who you should approach, ask yourself the following questions:

- What benefit does my company's product provide?

- What kind of people would I like to work with? Search for people like yourself. What hobbies or interests do you share?

- What financial benefits or career opportunities does my company provide?

And naturally:

- Who is the person I am looking for? Is he a manager or is she a housewife?

You will never be able to answer these questions perfectly, and outward appearance can lead to incorrect assumptions. But the only thing you have is a first impression of candidates.
95% of the most expensive car brand's costumers are not wearing a suit, and someone with a suit might also be a long-term unemployed, unskilled nobody.
So don't worry, deduce what you can from the appearance, but don't wonder if you sometimes get it wrong.
It happened to me that I talked to someone simply because there was no one else there to talk to. And then I found the perfect business partner in that person!
Keep your eyes open!

„The more humans are organized, the harder coincidence can hit them."
Friedrich Dürrenmatt

Tobias Schlosser about Target Groups:

"One day the board of directors sent out a memo that claimed that independent market analysts recommended recruiting women. This was a surprise for me, since I have only worked with men so far. It was difficult for me imagining myself to talking to female candidates about my business.
But naturally, it made total sense. Female team members would lead to female customers we otherwise didn't have.
It was exciting to create methods for this task. I thought it was important to redefine style on a high level while being effective on the other side.
I imagined the ideal female candidate around 30 wearing more or less business-style clothing.
My next mission led me to a Munich business district with a business partner. The surrounding companies provided (wo)manpower. While I was parking I noticed an energetic, young woman passing by.
So I gave it a try:

I: *"Are you from around here or working nearby?"*
She: *"Who is asking?"*
I: *"It might sound odd, but I just said to my colleague that you would be perfect for our team."*
She: *"Your team?"*
I: *"We are casting staff for a major German company and we are looking for dynamic, young women, who are up for a good job opportunity or a well-paid part-time job. May I ask what you are doing, job wise?"*
She: *"I am an intern at the moment."*
I: *"I see. Is it interesting to earn something in addition?"*
She: *"Always, but it depends on the job!"*
I: *"I am talking about team organization. Are you good with people?"*
She: *"Yes, I suppose so."*
I: *"I can't promise you anything yet, but here is my business card."*
She: *"Thank you."*
I: *"Is there a number where I can reach you?"*
She: *"Sure, I'll give you my home number: 089…"*

In a similar way I generated many numbers on that day."

Of course women are not the only target group you can focus on.

Tobias Schlosser and his experience with sporty people:

"In my opinion sportsmen are a great target group. Not only are they open for direct recruiting, they seem to be more qualified business men, since they have more discipline than couch-potatoes. They are used to motivating themselves and are used to defeats.

Since I am sporty myself it is easy for me to talk to like-minded people. Equal interests make everything easy.
As you want to build up a relationship quickly I suggest you to work within your interests as well. After all, it is more fun then.
That is why I often recruit in the fitness studio.
Yet jogging along the river Isar can also bring perfect recruiting atmosphere, such as on a sunny Saturday morning. I was taking a small break when I studied a man stretching himself intensively.

I: *"Hello, do you have a second?"*
He: *(laughs) "If it is only a second."*
I: *"Don't worry. I noticed that you are quite exact with your workout."*
He: *"Yes?"*
I: *"As you can see I like to keep in shape as well. And I am always looking for people that are taking care of themselves."*
He: *"Why?"*
I: *"I am an entrepreneur and am searching for dynamic and sporty people. At the moment I have two free positions in my company. What do you do for a living?"*
He: *"I work in an office. But I can't complain about my job."*
I: *"Good. Maybe there is still some time to earn some extra money. Is there some space left in you bank account?"*
He: *"Always. What exactly are you doing?"*
I: *"I am in a leading position of a company in the financial branch. I am looking for someone who can help me in the fields of coordination and team organization. Our specialty is pension funds."*
He: *"Sounds interesting. But I have to go on before I cool down."*
I: *"Sure, here is my card. Where can I reach you?"*
He: *"At home in the evenings."*
I: *"Ok, so I call you at home? 089..?"*
He: *"775431xxx"*
I: *"Then have fun. I'll call you.!"*
He: *"Ok, take care."*

PART 4

THE 2BEKNOWN SYSTEM

THE 2BEKNOWN SYSTEM CONSISTS OF 6 STEPS AND 5 MODULES

In every learning process single units, lessons or modules are simplifying the progression.

Just as learning a language starts with simple basics, direct recruiting can be learned best if you start at a low level and then progress.

Also, the motivation and the success in the first steps are creating confidence.

Beginners might find it difficult to start a conversation at all.

So as a first step, we should learn how to talk to people out of nothing, just in general, before we are going of to actual recruiting.

PERFECTION IN SIMPLICITY

Communication is everything. It is the basis of selling or recruiting! It is the essence of your business. There are recruiters who are able to create a firework of emotions in the heads of candidates, often achieved with very simple techniques.

Within years these recruiters developed tactics and techniques that make them successful.
But that's the problem!
Developing into "recruiting-champions" is good, but these skills are not multipliable. It is impossible to copy successful behaviour that doesn't match your own. That is why there was one big goal while developing the "2BEKNOWN method: It had to be multipliable. It had to be a "one size fits all"-method. And we found the answer.

There are two main aspects within the 2BEKNOWN method:

1. **Losing the fear of social contact**

2. **Improving communication skills**

These two points have a lot in common. They are strung together and it can be said that the bigger your fear is, the less you are able to communicate and vice versa.

It is like working out: without preparation and warming up you won't be successful. Don't forget that you want a long-lasting result. That is why we developed the model of 6 steps.

Take it easy at the beginning and have fun! Progress will lead to success, success will lead to progress.

"Bring simplicity to the top. Become a master of simplifying complex matters."
Tobias Schlosser

THE 6-STEPS MODEL

This model is the essence of the 2BEKNOWN method. Simple but efficient and tried out hundreds of times. This will be your fundamental basis for the training. Take your time (six days in a row, if you can), and practice one step a day. One step after the other will bring you success.

We suggest practicing each step 10 times. Of course, it does not hurt to do it more often. After six days you will be able to contact new people everywhere and anytime.

If you consequently practice you will notice that contacting will be like a well trained muscle, which almost works automatically.

STEP 1:   Smiling!

This is a very simple, nonverbal gesture. Just look into the eyes of anybody on your way and smile. No further action is required.

STEP 2:   Hello, how are you?

In the second step, you are simply saying "hello". Not a conversation, but more than a friendly nod: "Hi!"
You will learn patterns of reactions.

STEP 3:   What time is it?

A very simple yet effective way to get you into a dialogue is a neutral question. By asking for the time you'll get used to starting a conversation. Your opponent will answer openly. Once you get your answer, say "Thank you" and move on.

STEP 4:   Changing money

Ask someone for change. This procedure takes time and small talk is a natural reflex when standing together. Take a bill and ask for some coins. The next person could change it back into a bill...

STEP 5:   Compliments

From this point on you are talking to someone without an apparent reason. The candidates might be surprised. Make compliments about special features or clothing. As an example, talk about someone's shoes, a special tie or his nice car.

STEP 6:   Asking for directions

This may sound simple and it is a powerful and easy way to involve someone into a conversation. Ask for a cosy coffee place or a good restaurant; if you receive nice answers it is easy to go over to actual recruiting. Just drop another question after the description:
"Thank you. You described that so nicely, I bet you are working in the service department of your company." Now you are automatically in the middle of a business conversation by what seems to be coincidence.

Once you have worked your way through all six steps you are ready for professional recruiting. After completing the 6 steps you will have achieved the following:

- You are having fun

- Body language and moves are precise and calm

- Your voice is calm and clear

- Your words are well-chosen

- Your fear of talking to strangers will vanish

- You have talked to at least 60 people and might have some contacts already

- You are working organized and targeted

Using every day life situations enables you to develop conversations easily. You can improve your skills without attempting awkward recruiting methods in the beginning. So start recruiting out of "normal" situations.

You will notice that talking to strangers becomes a natural impulse. You'll get used to starting conversations wherever you are – at any time.

INTERNALISATION AND SETBACKS

It will be some time until the blood of a recruiter runs through your veins. The 2BEKNOWN method has the following training suggestions:

Give yourself one day per step. Within a week you will progress rapidly and constantly.

Day 1 - Step 1 (Smiling)

Day 2 - Step 2 (Hello!)

Day 3 - Step 3 (What time is it?)

Day 4 - Step 4 (Change money)

Day 5 - Step 5 (Compliments)

Day 6 - Step 6 (Ask for directions)

On the seventh day you are ready to implement your business, your text or to switch any conversation into your favourite topic: your business!

But what happens after a break? You are not in shape anymore and just didn't practice for a while. If that happened, please proceed like this: Let's say you started the 6-Step training, made it through all steps and recruited on the seventh day. But on day eight and nine you did nothing. On day ten you are starting at step 5 again, because for each day you didn't rehearse you are going one step backwards.
So you are going to pay compliments again, then ask for directions before you are simply recruiting again.
This makes sure that you are always working on direct recruiting as a concept.
And now proceed with your task for the day:

Step 1: Smiling

Have fun!

PART 5

THE FIVE MODULES OF SUCCESSFUL CONTACTING

Like any other social contact, direct recruiting is divided into five modules.

Module 1 = The Opening Sentence
Starting a conversation

Module 2 = The Reason
Explanation for starting a conversation

**Module 3 = Identification with
the Conversational Partner**
Building a relationship

Module 4 = Implementation of Your Business
Bringing your business into the conversation

Module 5 = Generating Contact Information
Exchanging contact data and closing
the conversation

While the 6 Steps method aims at decreasing your "fear of contacting", the five module plan brings you to a level of professional recruiting.

MODULE 1:
THE OPENING SENTENCE

The 2BEKNOWN-method relies upon standard procedures

> "Hello. I have a question: Are you from [your city]?"
>
> "Hi. Maybe you can help me out?"

Being in a party of two or more:

> "Excuse me, my colleague and I just made a bet: He thinks you are a banker, but I think you are self-employed."

It is amazing what can be achieved with finished sentences and structures, if they are implemented casually and with self confidence. Of course there is never a sentence for every situation. And the actual goal is to develop a social skill that is flexible and free, but predefined phraseology can be a great support.

That is why I suggest forming a couple of sentences to start with. Try them and see what is working for you.
If you are working with the same sentences patterns and reactions will appear. It will be possible to anticipate questions and answers. This can be a big advantage.

The other big advantage is that once you are fluent with your phraseology, you can concentrate on body language and voice. Your head will be free to analyze the reactions and respond accordingly.

The sentences above are just examples. It is always wise to use own phraseology. That makes it authentic because it matches you and your business.

MODULE 2:
THE REASON

If you are starting a conversation people will wonder why.
You should always provide a reason before they wonder. Explain why you are suddenly contacting a stranger. Don't forget, whoever you talk to will be surprised. It is best to use a positive feature for that matter.

Some examples:

"I just had to talk to you since you are wearing such flashy colours."

"You seem to be very self confident. May I ask you something?"

"You have such a positive charisma; I just had to stop you."

Grab out an important detail (e.g. his/her profession) and use it as your point:

"...is exactly what we are looking for!"

"People wearing individual clothing is exactly what we are looking for"

"Students are exactly what we are looking for."

"People with charisma are exactly what we are looking for."

Etc.

After explaining your reason you can go on and ask your first question. The first question should be within the same topic, or connect naturally.

For example:

"What does someone like you do professionally?"

MODULE 3:
IDENTIFICATION WITH THE CONVERSATIONAL PARTNER

It is important to identify yourself with the candidate. Show your honest respect for interest. Like always, the following recommendations are just examples and should be adjusted to the situation.

For instance, if someone is a farmer, ask detailed yet positive questions:

Recruiter:	"What does someone like you do professionally?"
Farmer:	"I'm a farmer."
Recruiter:	"And what are you planting?"
Farmer:	"Just corn."
Recruiter:	"I see, so you make every barbecue's side dish!"
Farmer:	"Well, you could see it like that."
Recruiter:	"Great. Listen …"

MODULE 4:
IMPLEMENTATION OF YOUR BUSINESS

Now you have contacted someone, explained why and then identified with that person, it's time for the exciting phase: your business! In this phase you are openly aiming at winning your conversational partner for you and your business.

Take the information you gained in previous modules and directly bring your business into the conversation:

"I am about to develop a new branch of my company here. We are in the wellness industry but I am searching for three people with experience in the banking sector to help me out with organising the team and improving the distributional department."

Or:

"I work for a large British company and am able to offer charismatic people like yourself career opportunities."

Just analyze your company's benefits and areas and adjust your offer accordingly.
Don't explain too much. You'll have time to describe your product and company in a second conversation. At this point it is more important to arouse interest.

In a business relationship (and any other relationship for that matter), each partner has interests: You want his name and number, he or she wants information on you and your business.
Of course this is never said openly. If someone does not get what he wants out of that conversation, it will end unsuccessfully.

MODULE 5:
GENERATING CONTACT DATA

After exchanging information with a positive outcome it is time to "wrap up the package".

Say what you are expecting! This can be:

- To come to the office for a second meeting

- To come to a job interview

- To meet at a café for a detailed talk

- To check out a online presentation

Whatever you want: get the telephone number at the end.
It might not be the best way to say:
"Give me your number, I'll call you." but it works.

More elegant is this solution:

Recruiter: "Let's meet for a cup of coffee somewhere, I'll explain everything then. Here is my business card. Do you have a business card?"

Candidate: "Yes." / "No."

If he has one, take it. If not:

Recruiter: "Then I'll quickly write down your name so I know who I am talking to."
[Write down the name]

Recruiter: "You are probably reachable on your cell, right? So 0 ..."

Candidate: "Uh...0176/123..."

This solution works almost every time. If the candidate did not introduce himself, ask for the name. That is the first important step. The second step can also be formulated with the alternative question technique:

Recruiter: "Is it better to call you at home or on your mobile?"

Candidate: "On my mobile."

Recruiter: "Ok. So 01..."

With this construction, 9 out of 10 people are completing their number. Of course, the 01 is how all German cell phone numbers start; you'll have to use the first digits applying to your state/region.

If candidates answer like: "I never give my number away." ask them for the reason.

In the history of direct recruiting, very rarely does someone actually call after receiving a number without giving away his own. Save your time and your business cards. "In that case I don't give my number away either" is a rude but probably fair answer.

EXIT

Now you have the number and can get going. No! Only leave if you or your conversational partner is in a hurry. Otherwise, talk for a while. Choose a personal topic. It is best to talk about the candidate himself.

Empathy is an important factor within your business. After this "connection process" you can leave. I would write down some notes on afterwards, so you won't forget.

THE "HEAVY FEET"- PROBLEM

After gaining some routine and after the first success, we encountered a problem we called "The Heavy Feet Problem".
This occurs mostly if recruiters are contacting in groups and in public places.

If you are contacting, whether alone or in the group, then contact!
You can grab a coffee to go and chat with your partners, but don't forget why you are walking through the city. Don't talk about how you are going to be rich one day – **talk to those who can get you there!**
To dream and fantasize is a wonderful thing, but simply dreaming won't get you anywhere.

If you are following your defined goals you will have plenty of time afterwards to chat and dream. I saw groups of recruiters wandering around the city, deeply involved in their conversations, without talking to anybody but themselves. Time flies and eventually they will return to their office disappointed.

Rainer von Massenbach remembers:

"I won't forget my first really successful direct contacting attempt. Tobias and I were waiting in front of a cinema. We got there earlier so I decided to catch some air. But after 10 steps I suddenly stopped. There it was, a shiny new BMW M3, the car of my dreams.
At this time, I had no car at all and got around by bus and train. The only vehicle I used was a shady old Ford I borrowed once in a while from my mother. And I knew it would be a while before I would be able to afford a car like that.
I slipped away into a day dream, imagining myself sitting behind the steering wheel of this black beauty. Suddenly a well-dressed man in his thirties walked straight towards the BMW.

With a majestic little beep the car opened and he was about to get in. I gathered my strength and started:

I: "Excuse me, but this is the car of my dreams. What does someone like you do to afford this car?"
He: (laughs) "It's a pleasure!"

Some explanations about his job were leaving his mouth, but I didn't understand a word of his lip service.

I: "Perfect. I am searching for somebody like you, who has already achieved something in life."
He: "I am always open for a business talk. But what exactly are we talking about?"
I: "Do you have a business card?"

I was happy that he didn't ask any questions and handed his business card to me. I thanked him and while already leaving (I was nervous since the first second), I said:
"I'll invite you to the office and then we can talk about everything. Sorry, I have to leave. Good bye."

This is probably not the perfect example of direct recruiting, but it was my first successful attempt on my own.

Tobias Schlosser about the usability of the 2BEKNOWN method in various fields explained using the personal training example:

Some time ago I helped a friend to set-up a personal fitness agency. Winning solvent costumers is essential in that business. I know trainers with plenty of qualifications but with no skill to market.

I had told my friend a lot about direct contacting and MLM and he was interested in that subject. So he asked me: "Tobi, do you think it is possible to get customers through direct recruiting as a personal trainer?"

I consider myself as an optimist so I immediately answered: "Yes!"

He looked at me with a shy smile and I could almost hear his thoughts: 'Could you show me how it works?'

Before he was able to formulate his question I felt I had to prove my enthusiasm.

As if being there for that purpose a tanned yet slightly overweight man was catching attention while refuelling his yellow Viper.

I took my friend's business card and walked over to the man to give it a shot:

> *"Hey! Nice car, I love it!"*
> He: *"Yeah. It's brand new."*
> I: *"The reason why I came here is because my friend and I agreed on the fact that someone with a car like that needs a personal trainer."*
> He: *"Wow. But as a matter of fact, I do have a couple of pounds I want to get rid of. But my job leaves very little time..."*
> I: *"Many successful people have that problem. What would you say to an effective and efficient personal training course?"*
> He: *"I don't know."*
> I: *"I see. Why don't we have a meeting, no obligations, where we talk about a schedule? Your body will match fit to the car within six months."*

He laughed out loud: "This has never happened to me before!"

I handed him my friends business card: "Here is my friend's card", I pointed over to my friend. "Let's have a coffee and talk about everything. Do you have your card ?"

He grabbed into the side-pocket of his horsepower-monster and handed me a business card. I became highly motivated. Even I was surprised that direct contacting can support various business types. Today that man is working out with my friend once a week.

Direct recruiting works in virtually every industry!

TALK TO THOSE
WHO CAN GET YOU THERE

PART 6

BASIC RULES FOR THE ACTIVE RECRUITER

PLACES

The huge advantage of direct recruiting is that it can be performed anytime and anywhere as long as there are people.
This can be at the zoo, in a café, or on the streets downtown.

You can also go to a big mall to find people, but don't forget to be prepared to talk to people in your everyday life. Just think about all the people you meet daily while getting to work, in the bus or at the gas station.
Wherever you are (with some exceptions such as the North Pole) there are at least 100 people within 50 miles worth talking to.

THE FIRST CUT IS THE DEEPEST

Even with some routine it will always be a little hard to make the first contact of the day.

If you have been contacting the day before, the problem is negligible, but after a few days of leisure you will notice a little devil inside of you.
Just start and the second and third candidate will be as easy as always.

Again, this is like a sport. When you start running, the first steps are always the hardest – no, to convince yourself to start running is the hardest part. So "warm up". Pick up the Six Steps module for that purpose.

TALKING TO COUPLES AND GROUPS

Talking to couples or groups is a bit tricky and not ideal for beginners. You have to be very professional and either pick out one person or manage to talk to everyone at once.

When it comes to couples, this is an absolute must. Job opportunities are often decided together. Leaving the partner out will make a bad impression.

On the other hand you will quickly find out who's in charge of important decisions, you you'll have to focus on.
You will learn how to cope with couples and groups after a while, but I would not start with those candidates on the first day of your contacting career.

LEVEL OF DISTANCE

There is a rather difficult point we can't answer for you: how should I speak to strangers?
"Hey man" or "Excuse me, Sir"?
You can find out what suits you and your business by analyzing these points:

- Your Company / Product

- Is your target group within a relaxed and open circle or are professionalism, quality and service more important?

- Costumers / Team Members

- Does it make sense to be equal among friends in your team or are you aiming for "high potentials?"

Analyze your business! But after all, the most important question is how you feel comfortable.

DON'T HESITATE

We often experience the ideal candidate passing recruiters with open mouths.
The recruiters face says: "I wanted to talk to him, but while thinking about it he already passed."

If you don't say anything, the candidate will be lost. If you are saying anything at all you have at least a chance.
Only if you don't say anything at all, the defeat is definite.

If you encounter problems like that, reflect on the system of six steps. Go one step backwards and ask the candidates for a nice café or restaurant, that will leave time to think about your approach and you are back in the game.

BODY LANGUAGE

Yes, again. Remember to act naturally. It is better to talk to somebody "coincidently" while walking than stiffly walking towards the candidate. Be personal. Individuality is important. Let the candidate have the feeling you are approaching him because of himself, not because you are performing a "promotional campaign".

Attitude is is key. Tobias Schlosser likes to start recruiting conversations over the shoulder, while passing a candidate. Rainer von Massenbach even let's them pass before he turns around "especially" for "this very person".

Have an open and relaxed body language. Wild and hectic gestures are to be avoided.

QUESTIONS, QUESTIONS, QUESTIONS

Sometimes a candidate is simply not interested after hearing your offer. How hard and unfriendly some candidates react does not matter: never "kick back".

Stay friendly and manage a "Good bye." Remember you are representing your business, not only yourself. In some cases you might represent a company or organisation of thousands of people. Don't ruin your company's reputation!
(If a candidate reacts in a harsh way, probably already ruined that reputation towards the candidate)
But those situations are rare. Normally questions like "What product are you distributing?" or "What exactly is the job about?" occur.

Another frequent question is: "Does it pay well?" This question should not be answered with numbers or something like "Twice as much as you are earning now".

If the candidate is interested a simple "I don't talk about money on the street, but let's meet in my office, I think we will agree on a payment" is better.

Be prepared. These questions will come. But I noticed that there are three to four questions before candidates are satisfied. In 90% of all cases these questions are the questions I just mentioned or similar ones.

BUSINESS CARD OR A PIECE OF PAPER?

A business card will be more professional and a piece of paper more personal. In large numbers it does not influence your accuracy, unless you don't feel comfortable with one of the options.

Try the following:

- Post-its
  This is something you could have along coincidently. Write down your number on one page and give it away.
  The candidate will have to think about where to put it since it is sticky. Meanwhile you can ask him about his data and write it down.

- Cell phone
  You can also use your cell phone and save the number in front of the candidate, making him important.

LIFE IS WAITING OUTSIDE

Direct contacting is not saved in your computer, is not in your office and not in this book. If you read this book to this page without having contacted at least 50 people: Go back to the module of six steps and finally start!
Only training can improve your skills, knowledge is secondary.

PART 7

INDIRECT RECRUITING

BASICS

Indirect recruiting takes time. It is about getting to know people instead of grabbing a number and leave.
The business is not the main topic and is supposed to get into interest without pressure just "by itself".

It happened to you before: You talked to a stranger and somehow the topic changed and you were talking about your business.
But how can such a situation be generated manually?

This variation only works in places where people are not moving for a while and can be involved in a conversation. This can be in a café, at the hairdresser or in a pub.

START

Indirect recruiting requires, just like direct recruiting, an opening sentence. Since the candidate isn't moving you can think about a sentence that suits the purpose.
Again, I would search for special features, habits or things you have in common with the candidate.

Rainer von Massenbach reacts on people using Apple like this:
"Oh. Do you prefer Apple, too?"
That is normally enough to start a conversation.

One more thing: It might not be worth mentioning, but be sure you know what you are talking about.

If there is nothing at all to talk about use sentences like this:

> "Excuse me, may I ask you something?"
>
> OR:
>
> "I watched you for five minutes now and I wonder what someone like you does for a living."

As an alternative, positively ask questions:

> "I just have to ask you: That neck-tie / dress / watch is really nice. I have been looking for something like that for ages. May I ask you where you bought it?"
>
> Or go one step further:
>
> "That might sound odd, but you seem so familiar. Don't you work for XY"
>
> OR:
>
> "Don't you have a hound dog?"
>
> OR:
>
> "Have you been at XY?"

Whoever you will talk to, such strange questions will arouse interest. The candidate will answer with "No. Why?" or something similar.

Now you have the chance to start a conversation.

"You look like someone I talked to at the last Christmas party."

OR:

"A hound dog destroyed my ball in the park last week. The owner looked a lot like you."

OR:

"I've been at XY and thought you had been sitting in front of me."

If the candidate laughs, you've won. It does not matter how weird or flat your opening sentence may be.
Try out whatever you can think of. Have you ever walked into a bookstore and asked costumers for a good book on the subject XY?

The only important thing is to be extraordinary, so be creative. If you are interesting, people will like to talk to you and contacting will be easy.

One of the most important things we teach in our workshops is recognising opportunities and taking advantage of them.

HOW DO I BUILD UP CONVERSATIONS?

Silence during a conversation is always a problem. Think about your next question or answer while the candidate is talking.

An example:

Recruiter:	"You seem to be so familiar, have we met before?"
Candidate:	"I don't know."
Recruiter:	"Hm. Maybe job-wise. What are you doing?"
Candidate:	"I am a graphic designer for alcatel"
Recruiter:	"Oh. Graphical designer. What field?"
Candidate:	"Mostly logos and business cards."
Recruiter:	"That's a good business, isn't it? Nowadays everyone needs business cards. How do you like mine?"

Here we go, now you are exactly were you wanted to be. Just ask questions or take one of the points the candidate mentioned and lead the conversation.

Candidate:	"I work for Siemens."
Recruiter:	"Ah, Siemens. A friend of mine works there."
OR:	
Recruiter:	"Oh, Siemens. Is it true that...?"

Include leading conversations in your training. It might seem difficult to lead a conversation in the beginning, but soon you'll be able to manage all small-talk conversation.
This technique avoids any uncomfortable silences, making the conversation enjoyable for you and the candidate.

Try to talk to five people for a while without selling or recruiting. Win a friend!

THE ELEVATOR PITCH

Wikipedia describes the elevator pitch:

An **elevator pitch** (or **elevator speech**) is an overview of an idea for a product, service, or project. The name reflects the fact that an elevator pitch can be delivered in the time span of an elevator ride (for example, thirty seconds and 100-150 words).

The term is typically used in the context of an entrepreneur pitching an idea to a venture capitalist or angel investor to receive funding. Venture capitalists often judge the quality of an idea and team on the basis of the quality of its elevator pitch, and will ask entrepreneurs for the elevator pitches to quickly weed out bad ideas and weak teams.

It is said that many of the most important decisions made on the floor of the United States's House or Senate are made „within the span of an elevator ride" as a staff aide whispers into a Congressman or Senator's ear while they head down to the floor to cast their vote.[citation needed]
A variety of other people, including entrepreneurs, project managers, salespeople, evangelists, job seekers, and speed daters commonly use elevator pitches to get their point across quickly.

Elements
An effective elevator pitch generally answers questions such as:
What the product is.
What it does for the buyer (e.g. the benefits).
Who you are.

In short: Formulate your business in one or two sentences that are reflecting the main benefits.

2BEKNOWNs elevator pitch is:

"We can teach you how to generate business contacts with fun and quality - anywhere, anytime!"

Keep an elevator pitch - your elevator pitch – in your mind. It is always a big help.

CLOSING - Indirect Contacting

Don't forget we want to win somebody's empathy. Forget your own benefits and provide valuable circumstances for the candidate (if your product serves that purpose, even better).
Help the candidate:

"Let's exchange numbers. Maybe there'll be future opportunities or ideas for the future."

OR:

"What you do sounds interesting. In my job I meet a lot of people. Maybe somebody will be in need of your services."

The important thing is to provide a benefit. Why do you need his number? The indirect contact is probably the most elegant way of generating contacts, but generating indirect contacts on a wider scale is impossible, even though these contacts are always valuable in one way or another.

FOLLOW-UP

Before we go back to direct recruiting, there is one more thing to be said about indirect recruiting. In order to arrange a second meeting, I highly recommend writing an email the very same evening. Include how happy you were about the chat.

Such an email could look like this:

Subject: About our little chat this afternoon

Hello ...

It was nice to have the chance to talk to you. It's always nice to meet kindred spirits. I've thought about you and already found some business opportunities you may be interested in.

Have a nice evening!

Tip: Include your website into the footer.

WHAT´S NEXT?

It is up to you to find the moment to bring your business into the relationship. In most cases this step comes naturally and you'll learn by time how to catch the right moment to start talking about it.

Rainer von Massenbach recalls a special contact:

"About three years ago I sat in a café enjoying a cold coke and worked on my evening lecture. I already had the habit of looking around wherever I was, searching for an ideal candidate.

That's why a woman in her late 20s caught my attention. She sat with her coffee and read a book.

I noticed her colourful purse and used it to open a conversation. As it happened, she was extremely shy and worked as an administratior.
We talked for a while and she told me that not being from Munich makes it hard to get to know people.

I decided that she could be valuable for my business, so we exchanged numbers and I promised to introduce her to some friends.
We met a couple of times and we had such a good time that I forgot to mention my business at all. (She has never become a team member of my business after all.)

I taught her how to fight her shyness and how to meet people – a great friendship was born. Today she is one of my best friends, knows a lot of people in Munich and, by the time this book is released, she will have returned from her honeymoon.
Want to know how she met her husband? In the very same café I started talking to her."

PART 8

FIRST STEPS

When starting to learn direct recruiting through the 2BEKNOWN method, you will progress just as you would by any other learning method: In the beginning you'll advance fast but once you've built up a good basis, improvements will become slower.

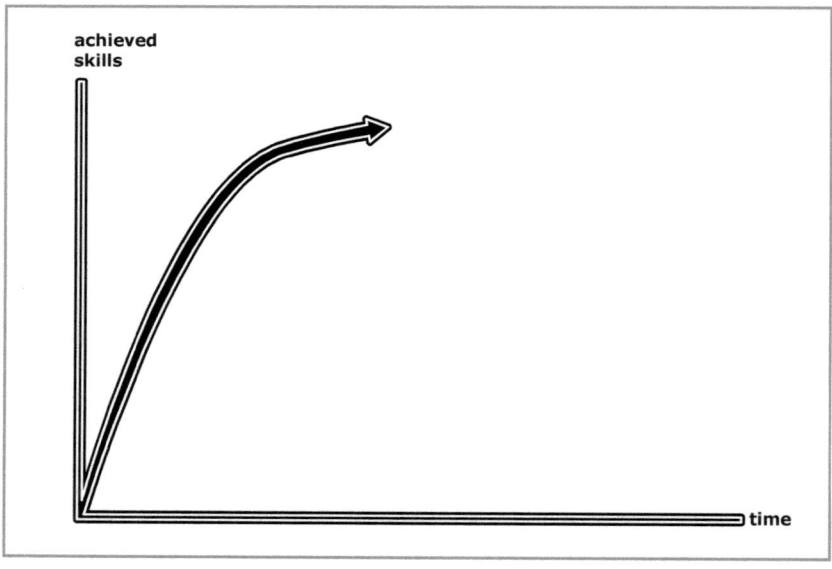

Direct recruiting is exactly like that. You'll learn how to work against your fears of contacting a stranger quickly and then you will work on your accuracy.

You'll make rapid improvements but then it will take a while to perfect your technique.

Your goal should be to train your "contacting muscle" into a state where direct contacting has become a reflex.

That ability is priceless and you shouldn't stop learning before achieving this goal. Of course, learning is never over, but you don't notice the training if it has become instinct.

This ability alone will lead to success. No "if"s and "but"s, if you are contacting your surrounding in perfection, you will be successful – in your business and in your private life!

All of our workshop attendees claimed that shortly after the workshop their businesses improved.
Having honed the skill of direct contacting you will be able to start a business anywhere you want.
We all know about the power of the word – it is time to use that power.

BECOMING A MASTER

Any brilliant chef started with sharpening knifes. Beginners have to learn their basics before they can use these abilities. So consider your training as what it is: Training.
It is more important to learn contacting itself rather than generating contacts. Even if you only gathered four contacts in a day, the twenty others you talked to are just as important to the learning process.
So, in the beginning put your business aside and concentrate on contacting.

It's like a video game. If a "game over" -screen appears, hit the start button and start again. If the outcome of a single contact is too important to you, you'll get nervous and you won't feel secure anymore, leading to bad results.
Don't worry: There are 6 billion people on this planet.

Have fun while you are learning and don't worry too much.

Once you are confident in the basics and a certain routine has been established you can bring your business back to the top of your priorities. By then,you'll be enjoying social interactions and this will enhance the results.

Action leads to reaction. Don't put yourself under too much pressure. Let go, enjoy the ride and improve after each attempt.

"EVERYBODY is recruitable. Just not by anybody at any time."
Tobias Schlosser

KEEP YOUR FAITH

One more thing: Some people learn faster than others. Never forget: everyone can learn direct contacting. Just promise yourself you will keep practising and you will get better. That's a promise. Remember how hard it seemed to learn things as a child.

Do you remember how you tried to learn how to ride a bike?
But you practiced and lost your fear, got faster and then had fun.
Corners became a thrill not a difficulty and now you don't have to think about them when riding a bike. You just do it!

I hope you are having fun with this guidebook and I wish you success in all the aspects of direct recruiting.

Sincerely,

Alexander Riedl

CONGRATULATIONS

You are through with this guidebook. But don't put it away. Read it again, if necessary. Take out required techniques or examples. We never stop learning.

Our team of experts are releasing, updating and informing all costumers through our email subscriptions. Our newsletter provides more free tips and tricks for a successful contacting career.

Sincerely,

Tobias Schlosser & Rainer von Massenbach

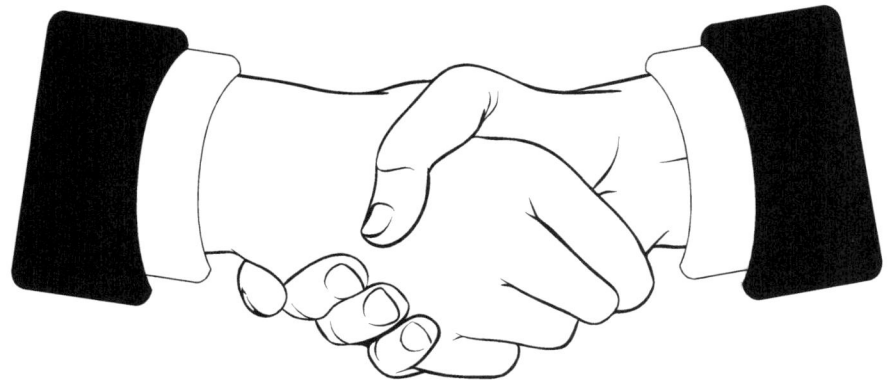

CONGRATULATIONS!

ISBN: 978 3 941412 03 3

Imprint

2BEKNOWN
2be GmbH
Oskar-von-Miller-Ring 33
80933 Munich
Germany

www.2beknown.de
www.direct-recruiting.com

Authors: Alexander Riedl, Rainer von Massenbach, Tobias Schlosser

Translator: Stefan Röhrl

Graphic Design: www.phuongherzer.de